a gift for

Peg

from

Jean

Having a loving relationship
with a sister is a wonderful
gift from our parents, and I
thank God.

A Helen Exley Giftbook produced under license for Hallmark Cards, Inc.

Published simultaneously in 1998 by Exley Publications LLC in the USA and Exley Publications Ltd in Great Britain. This edition published by Exley Publications Ltd in Great Britain and supplied to Hallmark under license. All rights reserved. No part of this publication may be reproduced or transmitted in any form or by any means, electronic or mechanical, including photocopy, recording or any information storage and retrieval system without permission in writing from the Publisher.

12

Edited and pictures selected by Helen Exley.
Pictures researched by Image Select International.
Typeset by Delta, Watford.
Printed in China.

**Exley Publications Ltd, 16 Chalk Hill, Watford,
Herts WDl9 4BG, United Kingdom.
Exley Publications LLC, 232 Madison Avenue, Suite 1409,
New York, NY 10016, USA.**

www.Hallmark.com

sisters

Selected for Hallmark by Helen Exley   ≣EXLEY

BOK4043

Sisters never quite forgive each other for what happened when they were five.

PAM BROWN, b.1928

Sisters remember things you would rather forget. In graphic detail. ... With proof.

MARION C. GARRETTY

*With a sister, one can never fear that success
will go to one's head.*

CHARLOTTE GRAY

Sisters stand between
one and life's cruel
circumstances.

NANCY MITFORD

When sisters stand
shoulder to shoulder,
who stands a chance
against us?

PAM BROWN, b.1928

The mildest, drowsiest
sister has been known to
turn tiger if her sibling is
in trouble.

CLARA ORTEGA

You know those television
commercials where somebody
stands in front of the mirror
and the mirror talks back?
That's what a sister is, a part of
yourself that responds to you.
You can see it and feel it.
This person you grew up with
and shared everything
with, who has your genes and
your blood and is so
much like you, yet also
different. I draw great strength
from that. You can't get the
same thing from friends.

SHIRLEY MASIEJCZYK, FROM "SISTERS"
BY CAROL SALINE AND SHARON WOHLMUTH

"WE'RE BEST FRIENDS"

Liza is my best friend and the only person I know I can tell anything to. She never judges me. It's really corny, but she's like a part of me.

LORNA LUFT

My sister is the friend who shows me what I want from other friends. She sets the standard everybody else has to match.

MICHELE D'AMBROSIO

I use the term [sisters] to refer to two women related by blood, most often growing up in the same house, in the same room, often sleeping in the same bed. As are all women, such sisters are taught by literature and culture to compete for the attention of men, beginning often with their father. Yet when asked to speak about their connections with each other, members of these pairs usually find themselves articulating a deep and turbulent bond, one that precedes and outlasts friendships, courtships, even marriages.

TONI A.H. MCNARON, FROM "THE SISTER BOND"

The desire to be and have a sister is a primitive and profound one that may have everything or nothing to do with the family a woman is born to. It is a desire to know and be known by someone who shares blood, history, dreams, common ground and the unknown adventures of the future, darkest secrets and the glassiest beads of truth.

ELIZABETH FISHEL

My sisters helped me to learn how to treat friends, how to be disinterested, to love who friends become, to work in groups with women, to support women. Theirs is a steadiness which mirrors what I think I have in my marriage – it grows and is lifelong. We are connected. They are the river which supports me and my other women friends as we float and swim along.

ANONYMOUS, FROM "THE SISTER BOND"

SULKS AND HUFFS

Sisters have it in their power to greet
anything you say with incredulity
and to kill any tale stone dead –
by shouting out the ending.
Sisters can do it
– but after you have dealt with them once
or twice in private
they learn to keep silent.

MAYA V. PATEL

Sisters annoy, interfere, criticize. Indulge
in monumental sulks, in huffs, in snide remarks.
Borrow. Break. Monopolize the
bathroom. Are always underfoot.
But if catastrophe should strike, sisters are there.
Defending you against all comers.

PAM BROWN, b.1928

We only argue about serious things, like if I get a stain on something and say it's not mine.

TAMERA MOWRY, ON HER SISTER TIA

To have a loving relationship with a sister is not simply to have a buddy or confidante; it is to have a soul mate for life.

VICTORIA SECUNDA

For all of us, being together, singing together brought the true closeness, the oneness that melded us one into another. It is our public image, that oneness. It's natural. We bring it from our home!

KATHY LENNON, ON THE LENNON SISTERS

We live in a
special space.
We thrive on
combined spirit.

**SARA CORPENING, ABOUT HER
TWIN SISTER MARY**

We are very lucky girls.
Always very *affinidad*.
Never disco dance
separate. Life for us is
pink. Happy color.
And together makes
us strong.

**HAYDEE SCULL, FROM "SISTERS"
BY CAROL SALINE AND SHARON WOHLMUTH**

When one sister is threatened or alarmed,
or when some ominous event looms,
it is as though an invisible thread
between our bodies has suddenly
tautened, and the others are drawn
towards the source of the twitching
disturbance. Any outside
threat possesses an unknowable,
arbitrary, swooping quality and we are
constantly on guard against
it, since any attack on one of us
constitutes an attack on us all, any breach
in our circle renders each one
more vulnerable. We always know, even
when apart, when any one of us
is in trouble.

POLLY DEVLIN

MIRRORS TO EACH OTHER

*What surprised me was that within a family,
the voices of sisters as they're
talking are virtually always the same.*

ELIZABETH FISHEL

*We are each unique, as is every creature
– but you are fashioned from the same
cloth as that from which I'm cut.
We sew on braid and buttons, frills and lace
– but the weave remains identical.
We are sisters forever.*

CLARA ORTEGA, b.1955

When I have Gladys in my arms and press her against my heart I know what love is, at least I know how it feels to love tenderly, truly, deeply, sincerely. My love for her can never change, and when I see how she comes to me in her little troubles or when she is tired and puts two tender arms around my neck and her head on my breast, it makes me feel that here is the pleasure of my life, here is someone who needs and loves to have me.

GERTRUDE VANDERBILT WHITNEY

You borrowed my stockings – and
spoilt them.
I borrowed your shoes – and
snapped the heel.
From earliest childhood we staged a
war over possessions.
"Mine. That's mine! Mum! She's
got my dress on!"
Dolls and gym shirts.
Tennis shoes.
Lipsticks. Knickers. Books.
Cassettes.
Even boy friends.
And yet –
Now that I have everything neat
and nice on shelves and hangers,
I sometimes long for you to come
around and rifle through my things
and say
"Oh look at this!
Can I just borrow it till Sunday?"

PAM BROWN, b.1928

*The young ladies entered the drawing
room in the full fervour of
sisterly animosity.*

R.S. SURTEES (1803-1864), FROM "MR. SPONGE'S SPORTING TOUR"

JEALOUSY AND LOVE ARE SISTERS

When we fought, like couples who've lived together for years, we knew the most tender nerve to strike. But when we decided to cooperate, we became a force to reckon with.

ELIZABETH FISHEL

What sisters really know is that they can fight with each other because they will always be sisters: they have a blood bond.

LAURA TRACY,
FROM "THE SECRET BETWEEN US"

When I look at Martha today, I see parts of myself and parts of my history. She has tested and helped me as no other person has, making me understand my limitations and my capacity for generosity. She is also my only immediate link to a life that is, for the most part, buried. We understand each other in a special way that defies the empathy of well-meaning friends. Whatever happens, we will be there to remind each other where we have been and how far we have come.

BARBARA LOVENHEIM, ON HER SISTER MARTHA

We disagree all the time. Remember things quite differently. Disapprove of one another's choices. Are maddened by each other's habits. But are sisters – and so tied into one another's lives – necessary in some strange way to each other's existence.
We stand on the same ground – and there, we are inseparable.

PAM BROWN, b.1928

No one knows better than a sister how we grew up,
and who our friends, teachers and favorite toys were.
No one knows better than she.

DALE V. ATKINS, PH.D

*She pictured to herself how
this same little sister of hers
would, in the after-time, be
herself a grown woman; and
how she would keep, through
all her riper years, the simple
and loving heart of her
childhood: and how she
would gather about her other
little children, and make their
eyes bright and eager with
many a strange tale, perhaps
even with the dream of
Wonderland of long-ago: and
how she would feel with all
their simple sorrows,
and find a pleasure in all their
simple joys, remembering her
own child-life and the happy
summer days.*

**LEWIS CARROLL (1832-1898),
FROM "ALICE IN WONDERLAND"**

BEING APART

It took years for us to find
our own pace,
to create a silence in which to
hear only the sound
of our own footsteps
and not feel that the silence
was a lonely emptiness.

POLLY DEVLIN

When you're around I laugh more
and I need that because I tend to
be so serious minded. You have a
way of finding humor in anything.

CORETTA SCOTT KING,
IN A LETTER TO HER SISTER, EDYTHE

We kick off our shoes, unloosen
belts and buttons, raid the
fridge, sprawl by the fire and talk
and talk. And talk.

MAYA V. PATEL, b.1943

It's hard to be responsible, adult
and sensible all the time.
How good it is to have a sister
whose heart is as young
as your own.

PAM BROWN, b.1928

I loved being a big sister so much that I took charge automatically. I went to their classes, I organized the shows in our living room, I fussed over their clothing and their hair. I included them in whatever I was doing, not to be bossy, I liked to think, but because that was what big sisters do.

BARBARA MANDRELL

A big part of paradise was caring for my baby sister.... I remember bathing, feeding, diapering, rocking, and hauling Michie all over the place until my little arms would just give out.... It was as if I were her mommy and she was my own little doll....

KATHIE LEE GIFFORD

As we wander the familiar [places], we talk of the common ground traveled together yet five years apart, the separate routes that have from time to time veered in opposite directions, only to converge again farther down the road. We talk of the differences that have been allowed to flourish, only to etch out and underline the similarities, the five years' distance between us that has actually narrowed the gap, so that we lose track of older and younger, exchange ages and places. We consider our roles in the family, once as sharply defined as salt and pepper. Now they have lost their borders, their constraints; there are no polarities, and, scrupulously, no favorites, each allowed her center stage, her retreat.... Had you happened to pass us walking along in the early-summer sun, you would have seen two laughing and chattering young women, engaged in that patois of strange inflections and private phrases, wrapped in each other's company and oblivious to the world.

ELIZABETH FISHEL

I claim the right as a sister to worry about you, to nag you, to stare very hard at your boyfriends, to criticize the length of your skirts, the cut of your hair, the shade of your lipstick.

I promise to cry at your wedding. Spoil your children. Send you vulgar postcards and ridiculous presents when I'm on holiday.

I will sleep on your floor if you need me. Donate a kidney. Organize secret parties for your special birthdays. Lend you money. And persuade you to spend far too much in the Sales.

I will praise, scold, rejoice and weep for you and stand by you forever.

... For all this is a sister's prerogative.

PAM BROWN, b.1928

*There is nothing I could
do, no disagreement I
could have that would
make my sisters not love
me. We belong to each
other and that is inviolate.
We each contribute to the
solidity of our bond by
being there when we're
needed. By carrying our
own weight.
You don't mess with that
kind of stuff.
You invest in it.*

CLAUDIA PHARIS,
FROM "SISTERS"
BY CAROL SALINE AND
SHARON WOHLMUTH

There are physical memories: washing in the bathtub, giving good-night kisses and snuggles, watching each other's bodies grow and change; scrutinizing who got bigger breasts and slimmer hips, who menstruated first, which one can eat anything and never gain an ounce, who's aging better, who has more wrinkles.... There are social memories: boyfriends, battles over clothes, shopping sprees, school plays, ballet lessons, family outings. And, of course, there are priceless emotional memories: heartfelt advice, unquestioned loyalty, late-night phone marathons; contemplating who was Daddy's little girl, who was Mom's favorite, who got the most attention, who felt rejected. The interweaving of these funny, joyful, angry, painful, and historic memories creates the foundation – solid or shaky – on which every sister relationship rests.

CAROL SALINE

*The passing years bring changes far greater
than we ever anticipated in childhood.
We drift with time, until one day we wake as
from a comfortable dream and find
ourselves strangers in a world we barely
recognize – a world of new technologies and
customs, fashions, speech –
and feel our own world lost and
half forgotten.
Until we turn and see our sisters and
our brothers, disguised like us in saggy, baggy
skins, and realise they are the same as when
we all were very small.
Here you are, a respected member of the
community, bespectacled and needing a pill or
two. A good act, convincingly presented.
But you and I both know that girl who laughs
at me through the slightly crinkled mask.
You are the one who climbs too high
and has to be fetched down.
You are the one who raids the larder,
draws horses in the margins of her school
books, fights the boys.*

PAM BROWN, b.1928

We are not only sisters. It is an amazing and sort of doubly strong association to be linked instinctively (and by environment, early life, etc.) and by one's desire and reason. It is a rare relationship. I feel as though you have leaned down and lifted me up to where you were so many times. At least if we have had things together your having them first or at the same time has helped me to realize and comprehend better what was happening.

ANNE MORROW LINDBERGH,
IN A LETTER TO HER SISTER, MARCH 1928

My sister Mary – best friend, soul mate, business partner – inspires me, awes me, encourages me. She is the first person I turn to in times of trouble, in times of joy.... Though we work together and live three blocks apart, we must speak at least twice a day on the phone. My boyfriend and her husband just don't get it. We do – we're sisters.

STEPHANIE ABBAJAY

*Thank you for hugging me when all the
world went wrong.
Thank you for reading to me when
I had measles.
Thank you for blowing my nose when I
was very small.
Thank you for holding my hand when
I was horribly afraid.
Thank you for taking care of me.*

PAM BROWN, b.1928

Four arms. Four legs.
One heart. One mind.
One soul. Always.

HAYDEE SCULL, FROM "SISTERS"

One's sister is a part of
one's essential self, an
eternal presence of
one's heart and soul
and memory.

SUSAN CAHILL FROM "SISTERS"
BY CAROL SALINE AND SHARON WOHLMUTH

ACKNOWLEDGEMENTS: The publishers are grateful for permission to reproduce copyright material. Whilst every reasonable effort has been made to trace copyright holders, the publishers would be pleased to hear from any not here acknowledged. POLLY DEVLIN: From *All Of Us There*, published by Blackstaff Press, © 1983 Polly Devlin. Reprinted by permission of the author. ELIZABETH FISHEL: From *Sisters: Shared Histories, Lifelong Ties*. © 1979, 1994 Elizabeth Fishel. Reprinted by permission of Conari Press. ANNE MORROW LINDBERGH: From *Bring Me A Unicorn:* Diaries and Letters of Anne Morrow Lindbergh, published by Harcourt Brace and Co. © 1972 Anne Morrow Lindbergh. Reprinted by permission of Harcourt, Brace and Co. SHIRLEY MASIEJCZYK Reprinted with permission from *Sisters*, essays by Carol Saline and photographs by Sharon J. Wohlmuth, © 1994, published by Running Press Book Publishers, Philadelphia and London. TONI McNARON: Excerpted by permission of the publisher from McNaron, T.A.H. (Ed) *The Sister Bond: A Feminist View of a Timeless Connection*, (New York: Teachers College Press, © 1985 Teachers College, Columbia University. All rights reserved.) CLAUDIA PHARIS: Reprinted with permission from *Sisters*, essays by Carol Saline and photographs by Sharon J. Wohlmuth, © 1994, published by Running Press Book Publishers, Philadelphia and London. CAROL SALINE: Reprinted with permission from *Sisters*, essays by Carol Saline and photographs by Sharon J. Wohlmuth, © 1994, published by Running Press Book Publishers, Philadelphia and London. HAYDEE SCULL: Reprinted with permission from *Sisters*, essays by Carol Saline and photographs by Sharon J. Wohlmuth, © 1994, published by Running Press Book Publishers, Philadelphia and London. GERTRUDE VANDERBILT WHITNEY: From *Gertrude Vanderbilt Whitney*, a biography by B.H. Friedman. With the research collaboration of Flora Irving Miller. © 1978 by B.H. Friedman. All rights reserved. Reprinted by permission of the Author's Representative, Gunther Stuhlmann.

PICTURE CREDITS: Exley Publications is very grateful to the following organizations and individuals for permission to reproduce their pictures. Whilst all efforts have been made to clear copyright and acknowledge sources and artists, we would be happy to hear from any copyright holder who may have been omitted. Art Resource (AR); The Bridgeman Art Library (BAL); Bulloz; Edimedia (EDI); Fine Art Photographic Library (FAP); Giraudon; Statens Konstmuseer, Stockholm (SKM); Sotheby's; SuperStock (SS). Cover and title-page: Mary Cassatt, Children on the Beach, National Gallery of Art, Washington, D.C./SuperStock; endpapers and background on title-page: © 2001 Hallmark Gift Books; p.7: © 1998 Walter Firle, A Good Book, SS; p.9: © 1998 Thomas William Roberts, Portrait of Gwyneth and Norah Langton Thompson, BAL; p.11: © 1998 Roland Wheelwright, On the Rocks, BAL; p.12: Edward Davis, Preparing for Dinner, BAL; p.15: Frederick Cayley Robinson, A Summer Evening, BAL; p.17: Charles Hodge Mackie, The Bonnie Banks O'Fordie, BAL; p.19: Pierre Auguste Renoir, Two Sisters, BAL; p.21: Isaac Snowan, Frolic, BAL; p.23: © 1998 Antonio Mahilum, Reyna Elena; p.25: © 1998 Peter Ilsted, A Young Girl Reading, Sotheby's; p.26: Ellen Hofman Bang, La Confidante, EDI; p.29: © 1998 Percy Harland Fisher, The Sisters, FAP; p.30; © 1998 Harold Harvey, On the Sands, Sotheby's; p.32: © 1998 Federico Aguilar Alcuaz, Three Marias; p.35: Michael Peter Ancher, A Beach Promenade, BAL; p.37: © 1998 Dorothea Sharp, Low Tide, St Ives, BAL; p.39: Alexis Harlamoff, The First Stitch, EDI; p.40: © 1998 Eugene de Blaas, The New Suitor, FAP; p.42: © 1998 Dorothea Sharp, On Lake Como, BAL; p.44: Michael Peter Ancher, A Beach Promenade, BAL; p.47: Pierre Auguste Renoir, SKM; p.49: © 1998 Charles Curran, Girls on the Heights, BAL; p.51: Berthe Morisot, The Cherry Picker, GIR/BAL; p.53: Mary Cassatt, Women Reading, BAL; p.55: © 1998 Istomin Constantin, Students, EDI; p.57 © 1998 Victorio C Edades, Country Girl; p.58 © 1998 Tito, The Dune, AR; p.61: Winslow Homer, Fisher Girls by the Sea, BAL.